Amazing Abilities
Of
Your
Magical Mind

Denisia Hockley

ISBN-13:978-1514329627
ISBN-10:151432962X

THANK YOU

To those who believe in my work and share all their
success stories.

CONTENTS

Denisia Hockley

PREFACE

We know that the first 4 or so years of life profoundly shape our emotional and relational circuits. The last decade has seen an explosion in the field of developmental neuroscience, its intersections with attachment dynamics, and its impact on how we nurture children (the fundamental starting point of every person). Professionals like Dan Seigal and Allan Schore come to mind. Yet there is another level, we also know intuitively that every 'good enough' mother (to use Winnicott's practical term) somehow manages to come through with the goods, even if she has never read a word of Dan Seigal. The Little Book Series (in particular Your Child the Little Scientist) values developmental science that confirms the nature and shape of "good enough" nurturance BUT deviates from typical ways of teaching so as to avoid getting lost in technical detail. The Amazing Abilities of Your Magical Mind goes even further by taking cutting edge scientific thinking and presenting concepts that are both exciting and challenging to your belief system.

Denisia Hockley

Amazing Abilities
of
Your Magical Mind
(Believing the Unbelievable)

Long long ago I discovered some amazing facts about the human brain; I engaged in and witnessed events that could be considered impossible, miracles, unbelievable or straight up lies; whatever!

Truth is your brain is capable of amazing things but social stigma, ignorance and fear of what one doesn't understand prevent you from realizing your full potential.

At that time I decided to get a university degree in psychology so that I could learn how to marry some of these 'unbelievable' phenomena with scientific credibility. The science of your amazing brain is now not only magical but largely measurable!

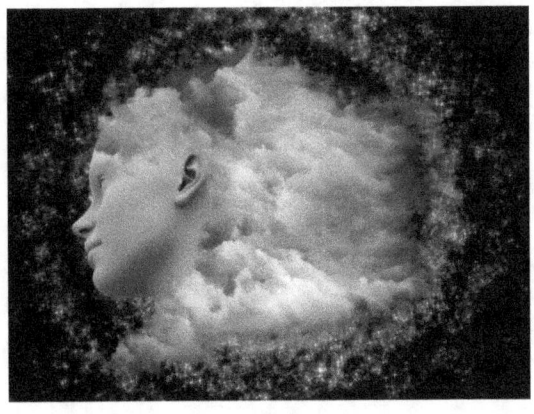

Still some things I am going to talk about will require you to suspend your disbelief, let go of rigid black and white thinking and always remember that more things in this universe are true other than just what we can see, feel, hear, understand and believe!

Of course if you need a more in depth, more technical perspective (of the exact same phenomena) research renowned experts such as Dan Siegel, UCLA expert on 'Mind-sight' or Dr. Alexander Everett who, back in the 70s and 80s, first played with Alpha brain activity and its impact on human potential.

So many of the events that society (even in this new millennium when people should be more open minded) still associate with mung beans and hippy beads, now have scientific backing'

My favorite example is of that little white switch on the wall near your doorway – go over now and flick it on...... magically your room fills up with light!
"So what" you say!
It's only electricity! No biggie!

Had you done that a couple of hundred years ago you would have been burned at the stake for witchcraft.

THINK ABOUT IT!

Brain Activity/Rhythms

I am going to refer a lot to brain waves/rhythms: once upon a time people would manually twiddle the knob of their radio to 'tune into' a radio station: if they had a high tech radio, late at night they might be lucky enough to pick up a short wave and hear a radio station in another country,

Essentially you twiddled your knob until your radio's wave pattern matched that of the radio station; a lot like matching up a fingerprint! As a psychologist if I start using words like telepathy, my cred goes out the window BUT you already know your brain runs brain waves of different frequencies   hmmm....

Now I am assuming you're fine with things like co-incidents, weird anomalies etc. Like when you think about your daughter and she calls; When you just 'know' something is going to happen, and it does. When you know who is on the phone before it even rings.... I could run off more examples but you know you have experienced 'not' being able to explain how you came to 'know' something or other!

Given that everyone has brain waves, and brains are far more powerful and complex than radios; doesn't it make sense that you just might be capable of tuning your brain waves into a similar frequency to that of someone close to you????? We will come back to this later, for now just open your mind to the possibility! Again you can find plenty of technical research to support this if you prefer reading long dry journals full of unnecessary jargon.

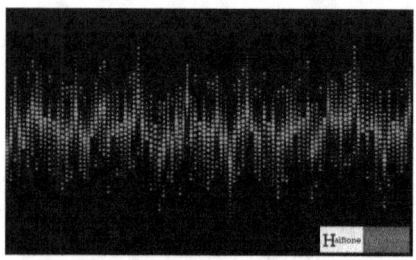

Sound waves

Brain waves

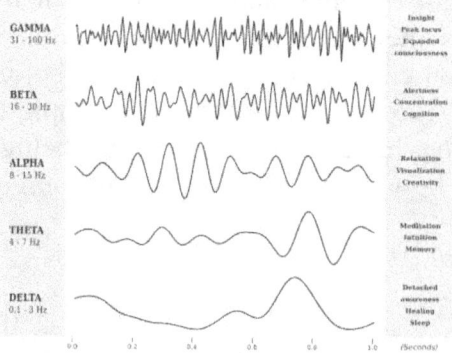

What are brain waves?   How do they operate? The science!

I am going to keep this simple as I just want you to understand your brain and how it works for you (you're not looking at going for a science degree here ok!) AND if you have read my other books you are expecting to have some humor and entertainment.

We can measure your brain waves on an EEG and we get graphs of squiggly lines that show the pattern and speed of your electrical fluctuations when you are thinking, learning, relaxing, losing the plot, falling love and anything else you do with your amazing little computer in your head. Since you (and your environment) essentially program your computer you have a lot of control over what it does for you and how it operates, but did you know you can train your brain waves (or rhythms'). There is a lot of exciting work going on in terms of neuro-feedback and bio-feedback, for use in a whole range of psychological and even psychiatric disorders but we won't go there just now. In my practice with Dr. Leon Petchkovsky we use lots of high tech (expensive) equipment to do neuro-feedback with psychiatric patients but it's exactly the same principle as what I am teaching you about understanding and working with your brainwaves.

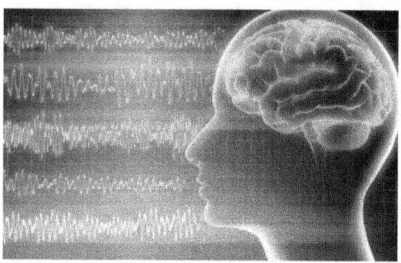

It can get rather technical as to which brain waves (activity) operate at the same time and frequencies etc. so the researchers and scientist reading this will have to put aside any anal pedantic tendencies they may have, I'm dumbing it down, NOT because my readers are not smart but because I don't want to bore them into a permanent 'delta' state (or coma).

Usually in my books I keep it light and simple BUT you need to read a little bit of the semi technical/science in order to believe the fun stuff coming later...(Actually this stuff is pretty cool too)

So starting with DELTA:

This is when your brain is running at around .5 to 3 Hz per second. (the one lower than Delta is when you're at 0 or less, that is flat line and we all know what that means [movie wasn't bad either]) You are in DELTA when you are in a very deep sleep, the type of sleep where if I woke you up you would feel like you had been hit by a truck, probably swear at me and collapse back to sleep. This is the sleep where your body does a lot of restore and repair work. If you are awake and running your DELTA you would be exhausted and probably somewhat depressed. Generally speaking, people these days do not wake up 'naturally', they use an alarm clock and wake up at the time dictated by their work and life commitments. For this reason they cannot control or predict where in their sleep cycle they will be when they awaken. Waking in the wrong part of their cycle could means lots of coffee and being a miserable grump all day. Many Jungians, and me, believe that this high Delta almost to Theta is when you have access to the collective unconscious, intuition, ESP and a kind of detached awareness. Interestingly enough we seem to be evolving slowly in understanding this vicariously through information technology: that is, we fully accept that the 'world wide web' (www.), 'cyber space' and now 'the cloud' are simply normal places where memory/information/ knowledge is stored 'outside of your physical computer/ hard-drive. That is, your computers collective equivalent. The collective consciousness of your mind is a place where memory, information and knowledge of all humans across time and space is stored and just like the "www", accessing this information is simply, or not so simple, a matter of understanding your brain. After all would anyone argue that the brain is the original and most powerful computer of them all.... Where do you think the know-how to build a computer came from?

DON'T GET CONFUSED: Brain states I will refer to as being in, either when you are asleep or wide awake can still have activity when you are not; we really don't need to get into that for this book. BUT you should know that babies and little people are operating in alpha and theta most of the time (that is why they are smarter and more together than we are).

I firmly believe that little people are born brilliant until we educate them to be as stupid as we have

become!

THETA: A really nice place to sleep, this is where lucid dreaming occurs (you can actually learn to influence your dreams, kinda cool (go get Inception the movie, for my money they got the ending all wrong but it is really interesting).

There are some really nice books on lucid dreaming (and some silly ones, so be selective) So, here in Theta we are talking about 4 to 7 Hz per second, 7ish is on the border of Alpha and that is the one we are going to mainly talk about later (Alpha and highish Theta). Low alpha – medium to high Theta is a lovely place to wake up and you can train yourself to do this with time and practice. Your body clock knows when the best time is for 'you' to wake up, unfortunately your work commitments, lifestyle and substances are allowed to override your body clock.

When you use my CDs (www.littlebookseries.us) Alpha/Theta is where you are going; it is where you learn really quickly and it is also where you store your memories (the bad ones are in there too but sometimes we need to access them to undo some of the programming on your hard drive). When you feel at one with yourself and your spirituality (whether you are religious or just centered and in tune with yourself- whatever it is for you) you will be essentially in this brain state. Work on your brain chemistry also takes place here, things like sodium and potassium are restored (a bit like topping up the fluids in your car – has to be done or your motor will blow up – your brain is much the same).

For those of you who take mini or nanna naps – 10 to 15 minutes theta/alpha sleep is like a super recharge, way better than sleeping in half the day which does not refresh you at all! So think of this as a place of heightened awareness and receptivity, going beyond what you think you know to what you really do know (access to the collective consciousness), and getting inspired and motivated (another good reason to wake up here).

And my personal favorites subject: ALPHA (note when I talk about alpha, that border over to theta is generally included). This is the brain state where your immune system is at its peak performance, and yet athletes are also in it when they break records and do things us mere mortals don't think we are capable of. People tend to associate being in alpha as a meditative state AND IT IS; meditative state does not necessarily mean sitting cross legged saying "uuuuummmmm" though. I actively access it a lot, both to meditate, get through exams and anything else where I need to draw on extra mental, physical or super conscious energy (see also The Little Book to Push through Pain).

Public speaking is something I really do not like, so my first method is to just get out of it. If that fails, or it is something really important, rest assured I will be doing a truck load of alpha rehearsal and put everything I have into staying plugged into alpha during the ordeal (I even listen to my own CDs). Like Theta ALPHA is the home of super learning.

Alpha: For pain, athletes and other stuff!

At university I used my alpha brain state to store all my abbreviated notes in my head, then during the exam I would close my eyes and read them… seems like cheating somehow! . (See also- using ALPHA to store stuff in your memory).

I hate hearing that kids at school get into trouble for 'daydreaming' this is such an important thing for kids (adults, grannies, all of us) to engage in; they are in alpha being creative and tapping into a rich source of sensory perception and reflection.

Alpha activity is associated with pain relief, addiction work and of course relieving anxiety, stress, and hypertension: My CD-therapies cover all these elements and some other cool stuff. Athletes already know the value of using visualization to prepare for events; well academic athletes can do that too.

When you are having a fear attack (formally known as anxiety) you use breathing and reassuring self-talk to slow your blood pressure, and everything else, down as well as to get into ALPHA.

By the way, alcohol screws up your alpha activity big time. Some of you might say you can get hold of drugs that do the same things but it is not the same, all drug highs come at a price (not just the $$$$$), they might fool you into thinking you are accessing super consciousness but they are actually making you rather deluded and somewhat crazy! Not to mention wrecking all this good stuff you already have access to with your natural brain. Seriously, mind altering drugs may seem good for a while but sooner or later your physical and mental health will have to pick up the tab and the cost will be steep. So stupid when you were already born with these amazing tools, you just need to learn how to use to the greatest advantage

BETA 14 -37 Hz (we used to think it went up to 26 but that has changed over the last few years/ they have also discovered GAMMA which goes up to 90+++ but I'm not going there either- you can research it if you want)

Essentially we need BETA but we do not need to spend as much time in it as people today tend to. It helps you get quickly into fight, flight, flee or freeze survival modes, it helps with highly analytical thinking but it drains your resources.

You don't leave your car in overdrive so why leave our brain in BETA.

 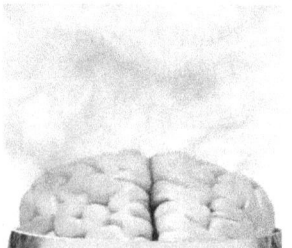

If you are always operating at a medium to high BETA level and then something happens to make you anxious, you then get flustered, speed up your breathing, your thinking and heart rate etc. and you soar to a much higher level of beta brain state.... You have been there I am sure... you probably called it losing the plot or having a meltdown. It can have a serious effect on your immediate health: So practice operating more with your slower brain rhythms' (i.e. move house to lower alpha) then when something does happen to make you 'anxious' and you start racing, chances are you will still end up in high alpha or low beta and be able to access the resources you need to take control of the situation and deal proactively with whatever needs to be done. Like so many things in life BETA has its place and of course you need to go there, I really do not need to waste your time teaching you to do this because you will always get more BETA brain activity than you really need. Again, you do not need to remember these technicalities but a brief understanding now will help knock some of the cynicism out of you for later.

How to cheat on exams!

OK I promised you some tips on USING ALPHA to store stuff in your mind (so you can 'cheat' in exams):

Our minds like good clear communication tools. I used to do a bit of a memory demo at seminars years ago. People would call out all sorts of random things, I would be blindfolded and have my back to the group and the facilitator would write items on a whiteboard which I of course could not see.

Absolutely no tricks, no sleight of hand just me and my memory techniques using brain capacities that you also have. The items would be numbered and he would say them a couple of times. People trying to be smart of course would make the things really complex, I remember one guy using as one memory item " 586 thousand teenage boys wearing green hats and having 98 zits on their face" and another called out "a blue ford station wagon with 2 flat tires, purple seat covers and being driven by a blonde with green streaks in her hair"- thing is, while they thought they were being difficult they really made it so much easier because our brain loves picture with color, humor and variety; once you take a snap shot of all of that and hang it in your brain it will stay forever almost (see section on RAS/radar).

The Techniques

- Get into your Alpha brain state by doing the breathing and relaxation exercises (Annihilate Anxiety goes into detail if you're having trouble with this: but keep it simple)

- Visualize memory hooks numbered from 1 to as many as you need: make sure they are attached/linked to each other (physically so when you see them in your mind they are connected).

- Take each item to be remembered, convert it to a picture, visualize it, see it in your mind, and attach each one securely to a memory hook.

- When you need to remember these items, go into your alpha breathing state with eyes closed , pull up the picture of your memory hooks and all your items will be there where you left them.

When you are revising your exam notes, use lots of colors, different fonts, drawings and acronyms, use a lot of humor, cartoons etc. AND really important.... When you are writing this stuff (I personally think handwritten is best) make sure you connect the dots, that is, you want one idea or concept to link to the next one in your notes and in your head (and later in your mind picture) from the beginning word or picture to the next, (on your memory hooks) make sure you draw a connecting line (in your notes and in your mind's eye) so that you have a 'chain of memory'. Example: I am asked a question about stages of something and I know step one so I close my eyes and go to a picture of step one in my mind then I follow the link, kind of a "this bone is connected to that bone" process. Try it! It works!

WHAT IS TRUTH?
PERCEPTION IS REALITY?

What is in your head affects your world way more than the things in your reality.

A client once told me she had grown up believing/remembering being raped as a child: That this had controlled and directed her sense of 'Self' (see Little Book for Reviving Relationships & Salvage Self-esteem). She now wondered if it was true or had she somehow imagined it. The fact is, whether 'it' had happened or some set of circumstances that made her think it had, was now irrelevant. It was 'her truth' 'her perception' and therefore her reality. Her memories were real enough and they were on her hard drive! Those memories were part of the foundation for her core beliefs.

SOME INTERESTING INFO ABOUT YOUR BRAIN.... IF YOU'RE HIGHLY SKEPTICAL YOU MAY STRUGGLE WITH THE NEXT COUPLE OF PAGES ....THE 'R.A.S' I MENTIONED EARLIER

RETICULAR ACTIVATING
SYSTEM (let's call it your Radar)

In very simplistic terms the 2 main functions of your radar are to SORT DATA & SEARCH FOR ANSWERS!! Every 1/18th of a second your brain is subjected to 1850 bits of information, internal sensations such as a pain or an itch and external stimuli from your 5 senses, (or 7 according to parapsychologists) that is 33300 per second,,,,,,,, what do you think would happen if you had to try and consciously process or attend to all this information…..???????????? Just under 2 million bits of data a minute…….. Sensory overload! Meltdown.!

YOU WOULD MOST LIKELY GO INSANE

RIGHT??????   (I have some theories in terms of how this relates to schizophrenia but that would have to be another book)

Obviously some of this information is more important to you than the rest......but how does your brain know what to pay attention to and what to store away in your subconscious.

Imagine you have a super-efficient personal assistant who holds all your incoming calls and only puts through the ones you want, or need to attend to....

Your RADAR does that, but on a much larger scale...It sorts the important stuff (let's call it D.I.P.I) into your conscious awareness and the rest (the NON-DIPI) into your subconscious (Some part of your dreams may well be your PA sorting info you need to keep and other stuff you do not)

So what does **D I P I** mean?

HOW ABOUT **D** for DANGEROUS...... someone is driving toward you, on the wrong side of the road at 80 miles an hour I would say you would want to notice that in time to get out of the way ...Right!

If you're watching TV and you have a toddler playing on the floor, and she is about to stick a fork into the power outlet... you might want that to catch your eye too!
D.......... things that threaten your safety ....

You can train your Radar to locate and define what is important or threatening to your survival. Actually it is more like training your mind "NOT" to interfere with what it already wants to do for you.

- Meditate
- Focus/Visualize
- Follow through

Teach yourself to divert focus from pain to another target. "Mentally attending" to what you want more of and refusing to focus on what you do not want.

A perfect example of your Radar at work is when you are driving your car, probably the most, potentially, dangerous thing we do on a regular basis! The music is loud; the kids in the back are playing. You may be talking on your phone, there are stimuli all around, ADVERTISING bill boards designed to attract your attention, designed to attract your RADAR by using pleasurable and novel stimuli!!!

With all that going on you are still, for the most part, able to pick up on dysfunctional engine sounds, the feel of an under inflated tire, MORE IMPORTANTLY YOU HOPEFULLY MANAGE TO NOTICE AND BE PREPARED FOR A CHILD ABOUT TO RUN ON THE ROAD OR A SPEEDING CAR THAT SEEMS TO COME FROM NOWHERE...

………..OR DO YOU?????????

Please please take warnings more seriously, about using cell phones and other stuff while you are driving! Your world could be seriously changed in a matter of a few seconds! Especially when you take your radar off auto-pilot and focus your attention on the wrong things! Your radar is great BUT only if you use it! Like everything else I have taught you, your magical mind has to be respected, used and understood if you want the benefits!

If, over time, you have become lazy you can now "RE TRAIN" your Radar to pay more attention to potentially dangerous events over other interesting stimuli

ONE OF THE REASONS ALCOHOL IS SO DANGEROUS TO DRIVING AND OPERATING MECHANICAL EQUIPMENT IS THAT IT INTERFERES WITH RADAR FUNCTION

OK 'D' is for Dangerous!

SO WHAT ABOUT THINGS THAT ARE IMPORTANT TO YOU….I
Mothers of young babies can often sleep through all sorts of noise but the moment their baby stirs they are awake

You have just decided you want to buy a new car, a hot black Mustang with leather upholstery, very cool. Once your brain, your Radar, has a picture of what it is you want, you will start to notice every similar car that you pass.

In fact if you listen to your 'intuition', your Radar might even take you to one you drove past a week ago but at that time it was not Important to you!

'INTUITION' IS STILL A CONTROVERSIAL SUBJECT. Again--- people fearing what they don't understand!

One 'SCIENTIFIC' theory about Intuition is that it is auditory responses OR little messages to us, generated by our Radar,

I is for Important!!

P is for Pleasure   You are at a conference with 2000 suites discussing Quantum Physics and as scintillating as the conversation is, your attention is drawn way across the other side of the room to a tall, dark honey with big brown eyes, broad shoulders, big arms ....oops.. that would be my Radar,   ok so YOU notice a cute blonde in a short skirt OR the last piece of chocolate cake on the banquet table!

Anyway, our tall dark honey in the corner takes off his shirt and jacket and reveals a huge tattoo of Homer Simpson on his chest! Male or female, most people's Radar will be drawn to that because it is out   of   the   normal   scope   of   perceptual stimuli….Interesting.

D I P I. Dangerous, Important, Pleasurable and Interesting data is picked up by your Radar and brought to your attention while all the rest goes into your subconscious (remember that nearly 2 million bit of information per minute!)

The Power of attraction

Your mind: like an iceberg
is so much greater than you can perceive.

Remember I said we were going to talk about WHY we do not say (use the words) things are hard (when they are) or I can't etc. etc. Your Radar actually is guided by your words (and the pictures in your head) so this is why you need to speak in the positives, it just takes some practice….Again this is 'science' not alternative! Not new age! Your mind is like a magnet, attracting whatever you think most about! And yes, we get it, it IS hard to say you feel fine when you actually feel like crap, but do it (or if you can't then say nothing). Mostly the person asking how you are doesn't really want to know! (fake it till you make it)

You should believe it, you have done in often enough (usually to bring about what you didn't want though). Remember how your mum told you over and over and over what was going to happen….. That's some pretty heavy conditioning so of course those things tend to happen. She kept saying it; you kept visualizing it and - Bazinger!!!!!

This concept is about communicating with your brain/computer: If you keep putting pictures in your head of what you want to happen (or what you don't) you are saying "hey brain, make me do whatever it is I need to do to bring this picture into reality". It's like 'googling' for your brain. If you have ever tried to ride a motor bike you will know the consequences of looking straight at what you do not want to smash into; golfers know not to focus on the water or the trees because that is where the ball will go.

This is totally consistent with the original concept in **Little Scientist** "Focus on what you want and ignore what you do not want!" It is a powerful key if people would just use it! Just reading this stuff won't change your life:

Using it WILL!!!!!!!!!!!!!!!!

Your radar does other cool stuff too (and the scientists out there reading this are going nuts at my seriously simplified version of all this!)

One other cool thing it does is to answer questions and attend to instructions you give yourself!

YOU HAVE BEEN DOING THIS ALL YOUR LIFE, HOWEVER IF YOU HAVEN'T KNOWN HOW TO ASK CORRECTLY YOU MAY HAVE GOTTEN RESULTS YOU DID NOT WANT.

What we fear we create!....to get the best from your Radar you need to know how to ask positive powerful questions instead of negative destructive ones.

GETTING WHAT YOU WANT IS EASY BUT FIRST YOU NEED TO KNOW WHAT IT IS! AFTER YOU KNOW, THEN YOU HAVE TO USE YOUR TOOLS! USE YOUR MAGICAL MIND!

Self-fulfilling prophecies may come from you talking yourself into situations. Ask your Radar (your mind) to help your find the perfect job at the perfect time...or to guide you to the person you want to spend the rest of your life with....(remember to make a picture for your mind to refer to) HEY TRY IT! WHAT DO YOU HAVE TO LOSE????

If you keep telling a child not to fall on the stairs it immediately thinks and creates a mind-picture of the stairs and falling, so what eventually happens...?

It is said that the optimist sees the glass as half full and the pessimist sees it as half empty..... Actually they both SEE the same but they interpret and verbalize it differently. The optimist says the glass is half full, or this cold is temporary I will be fine by tomorrow – or I am going to get this job! The pessimist, with the half empty glass might say, I have the flu and I'm dying OR why can't I get the perfect job for me…

Sometimes we confuse our brain by asking for one thing then asking for a second thing that is inconsistent with the first. So when you don't get something, realize that it may be for the right reason ie: not getting the job you think you want might leave you free to get the one that is best for you.

Great, but how do you get to this wonderful brain state……?

You can start learning to control your brain rhythms by controlled breathing – and self-talk - by practicing correct breathing on a daily basis it will eventually become automatic –

It may not happen overnight, but it will happen!

People have told you for years to just 'BREATH' but has anyone ever explained just how powerful correct breathing is……? Did you know that breathing affects your brain rhythms, your release of hormones and other natural chemicals….as well as your heart rate and blood pressure…? (See The Little Book to Annihilate Anxiety). Proper breathing is slow, deep and from the abdomen.

Formal meditation is as simple as systematically relaxing your body from head to toe by using slow deep breathing and using imagery (visualization) to guide your mind to a calm peaceful place; usually a scene in nature. The CDs I have created will take you there easily – all you need to do is use them on a daily basis, do not over-think or make a chore out of it – just lay back and let it work for you. The less you try the easier it will work for you!

Understanding and using VISUALIZATION: Often people will say that they cannot visualize or see colors; this usually means they are trying too hard or expect something more complex. You can remember what a red fire truck looks like, put a picture of a red fire truck in your head now: You are visualizing!

Remember I told you your mind works with pictures/images rather than words; when you think about falling down the stairs you actually run a very quick, mini movie of that event in your head. Some people spend their entire life using negative words to create negative images; I am sure you can remember your parents, or some other significant person, 'conditioning' you with words like "your always late" "your lazy" "you can't do X so there's no point in trying".

You grow up running these programs (movies) and over time you can be conditioned to behave accordingly. Take a few moments to think of your own examples of how you obediently live out something that you were told many times as a child. (You really need to read Little Scientist if you haven't already). As an adult you now come up with your own negative conditioning. Have you used expressions like "I always meet the wrong guy" "I never win anything" "I am always sick" "All girls cheat on me". You now know and understand how you have used visualization and negative programming very effectively in your life; albeit to create things you actually did not want.

Now you need to turn it around and use it to enhance your life: change your words, change the images and in time you will see a change in the consequences. Combining meditation with guided imagery means getting into a special place in your mind and purposely running movies/images of what you want/intend to happen or come into your life.

Maybe see yourself in a scene where you are with the girl of your dreams, see the family you want, maybe the house or whatever that represents happiness to you. Create this picture (and others for other goals) and hang it in your mind.

That is, imagine a wall, gallery, whatever, where you keep pictures of you goals and dreams. Whenever you meditate or even just take a few moments to relax, look at these pictures and reinforce that these things will in fact manifest!

AS I HAVE SAID BEFORE: Even if you are a non-believer, even if you do not except the mountains of science that supports this stuff; WHAT DO YOU HAVE TO LOSE!!!!!! The alternative is just keep wasting your magical mind power on creating the same disappointments in your life that you have been complaining about all this time!

A common problem exists where people do all the right meditation, visualization etc. etc., they may even put quality time into it. BUT then throughout the day they go back to entertaining doubts, what ifs, fears… that is…. back to focusing on what they don't want. Like most things, you must 'follow through'.

You often see people meditating with their finger and thumb together, I wonder how many of them actually know why they are doing that or are they just copying all the cool Zen meditators. I do it, and in some of my CDs I guide you through a process for setting it up as a mental trigger device. There is nothing magical about that particular action except it is simple, portable and serves a purpose. In hypnotherapy and meditation we use anchors, triggers etc. which are small cues to remind your brain of a more complex command. For instance I may take you through a detailed anxiety meditation at the end of which you tell your mind "whenever I put my finger and thumb together like this I will remember to………………etc. etc." After a while all you need to do is one simple little action and your brain knows exactly what you want from it. Look closely at some of those loud, confident motivational speakers and you will often see a little finger and thumb action discretely taking place.

Students use it to remember notes. Call it crazy if you like but again, what do you have to lose, it's organic, non-toxic, costs nothing and most definitely 100% fat free.

Finger and thumb technique, other triggers devices, cues, communication with your mind!

Stuff you can't explain! How you knew who was on the phone! What someone close to you was doing when you theoretically could not have known....

How do you know what to believe? Skeptic or realist? Psychic or nutcase or just plain fraudulent? Or maybe, just maybe, there are many things that while being unbelievable are also true, despite YOU not believing! Many people have been proven to know things that they have no way of knowing; you can chose to believe or not; UNLESS you personally experience this phenomena in which case you have no choice but to believe in the unbelievable .

Let me say again, there are way more facts and phenomena influencing your planet and your world than just what we can perceive and sometimes believe. It is ok to have some healthy skepticism, especially if someone is trying to sell you something or talk you into a major life change. On the other hand having an open flexible mind and leaving the door open for things that, even if you do not understand, it is possible that others do and that maybe 10, 50 or 1000 years from now will be common knowledge (fact even). You only have to compare many of the things we currently take for granted with how they would have been thought of in the long long ago of man's existence.

In the 1500s there were those crazy renegade medicine men who talked of invisible aliens invading the human body and being the cause of illness and death; they thought you could kill these imaginary creatures with soap and water! Of course today we know it takes antiseptics, antivirals and antibiotics to kill 'germs' 'infections' and 'viruses". !! I wonder what happened to the first caveman to light a fire. The natives probably used it to burn him at the stake.

I find it ironic that even today, people ridicule the concept of communicating from one human mind to another and yet those same minds created TVs and computers that send amazing images and sounds around the world in no time at all. In fact we are so used to these miracles that we complain because it took a whole 2 minutes to download a movie! It was hard enough believing all those actors and musician could fit through the cable and now they do it Wi-Fi!

Take your IPad back to the 17th century and see what reception you get from the natives! One century's magic is the futures commonplace technology! AND it all starts with a brain, a thought from which come theories, then skeptics and eventually Magic! 'Lucy' is definitely my favorite movie right now….go see it. Is it Sci-Fi OR Sci-soon-to-be-Fact!

Kirlean photography: True or false? People have been talking about auras for a long time and I'm not so sure about 'some' of those people   BUT remember the light switch!

We know we are essentially energy (electricity maybe/whatever) and there are dozens of experiments you can do to 'prove' that you do not end at the surface of your body. That's not rocket science.

Kirlean photography refers to a camera being able to take pictures of energies (or auras if you like) around living matter (people, plants etc.). I am as big a skeptic as anyone else in terms of reality and knowing what can be fudged. Statistics are the worst because everyone believes you if you quote a stat (even if you made it up on the spot).

Even statistics that come from respected research can be manipulated to prove almost anything (true or false) that is why to gain credibility research needs to be repeated and tested over and over before we accept it as most likely true.

Bottom line is I can't say definitively from my own personal research or knowledge if Kirlean photography is for real, BUT I can say the concepts fit well with my understanding of the human entity, energies and connection between living things.

My own theory (consistent with that of Carl Jung and many others) suggests that we have layers of energy/mental existence that go even further than what Kirlean photography suggests.

I'm not going to get into the 'God' debate (that would be a whole other book) but clearly there is some sort of superior element of (our) consciousness:

So think of it as a mainframe computer that holds all the knowledge, learning and evolutions from the beginning of human development. Each of our brains is like a mini computer with a Wi-Fi connection to the main frame. You have access to all that information but you need to be I.T. smart to get into it. You have to have a good signal and the skills to use the programs, software etc.

And you need to interpret the data. You have the equipment but as I have been saying throughout, you need to put in the effort to get the best results.

Everything begins with a thought, then comes a theory, then the inevitable skepticism to hold it back a few generations until finally it births into scientific fact!

Actually science can lie too, but humans are totally going to believe a scientist over a parapsychologist!

AND they will believe 'statistics' over either!

At the end of the day there are very few free rides, you have to use stuff if you want the benefits!
We all have access to this amazing 'machine'
But unless you drive it out of the garage it is of little value to you!

Fact Fiction Believe Doubt ...
.... But What If ??

So recently I have had my disbelief system challenged: I do not believe in ghosts, spirits or any form of dead people coming back.... BUT always an open mind...

When I see these so called phenomena on TV I really believe it's all a set up.... BUT now I have a very reliable friend who not only claims firsthand experience but has shown me some, shall we say, though provoking photographs he took.... So as an open-minded, scientist and in this case, non-believer; I now need to go with this person to see for myself.

When I have my findings I will blog on wordpress.com on my 'Amazing Abilities of Your Magical Mind' page... to check back there from time to time for updates.

So re read this book, highlight the bits you need to work with and start using more of your brain's potential:

Just Do It

Daily practice, living it!
You meditate 30 minutes every morning
And again at night!
You visualize! You ask! etc. etc. ,
So why does your life still suck??
Effort! & Follow Through!

Bibliography

Albert Ellis (1995)Clinical Applications of Rational-Emotive Therapy

Albert Ellis (1995) Handbook of Cognitive Therapy Techniques

Elizabeth Hills (2006) Getting in touch with your inner bitch,

Jon Kabat-Zinn, (2008)Full Catastrophe Living

MacKay & Fanning (2002) Self Esteem

Manual J Smith (2000) When I say No I feel Guilty

Michael J Free (1999) Cognitive therapy in groups: Guidelines and resources in practice

Rudolph Dreikurs (1985) Happy Children

Illustrations & Photography provided by family, friends: Fotolia, Istock & Dollarphotos

Please visit www.littlebookseries.us

"The Little Book & CD" series.

 Your Child the Little Scientist

 The Little Book to Revive Relationships

 The Little Book to Annihilate Anxiety

 The Little Book to Push Through Pain

 The Little Book to Defeat Depression

 The Little Book to Salvage Self Esteem

 The Little Book to be Physically Phabulous

 Amazing Abilities of your Magical Mind

CD therapy

 Anxiety  Alcohol

 Drugs  Depression

Smoking  Self Esteem

 Relationships  Pain

Abandonment  Sleep

 Anger  Health

Magical Mind

THE AUTHOR

Denisia Hockley
Clinical Psychologist/Psychotherapist/Author
Dip.Psy.,BA.,BSc.(Hon)Masters Mental Health (Psychotherapy)
Registered AHPRA: (Australia): MAPS Clinical College (Australia)
Member APS (American Pain Society)
Member Association of Independent Authors USA
www.littlebookseries.us
littlebooks2013@gmail.com

Denisia J. Hockley is an Australian Clinical Psychologist: Since 1998 she has worked with everything from general anxiety and depression to victims of trauma and abuse to everyday families struggling with typical life issues as well as those with clinical psychiatric disorders. In 2010 she worked in California specializing in clients with chronic pain issues. As a therapist, she has worked in outback aboriginal settlements, men's correctional facilities, addictions programs and private practice/s. Her style is laidback informal, and solution-focused. As well as CBT, Psycho-education and other general practices she is a qualified psychotherapist and also works with Prof. Leon Petchkovsky with his Neuro feedback clinic. An ex-policewoman, she has had a colorful and diverse career. Denisia's specialties include Complex Post Traumatic Stress Disorder (CPTSD) & Developmental Trauma (non-organic) in adults and adolescents: which result in anxieties, depression, personality disorders, relationship and self-concept difficulties as well as many physiological symptoms including pain and gastrointestinal disorders.

She is most passionate and fascinated by brain science and as she terms it... The Amazing Abilities of our Magical Minds, She has written a number of book including *Your Child the Little Scientist:* Her Little Book Series address every aspect of life, health, happiness, and mental wellbeing and can be obtained as E-Books at www.littlebookseries.us She also has a series of CD therapies covering Sleep/Addiction/Health & Weight/Anxiety/Depression and more: Visit her site for more information on these.

Denisia Hockley